# This is a True Story

Princess Zanele Nkosi

Published by New Generation Publishing in 2016

Copyright © Princess Zanele Nkosi 2016

First Edition

The author asserts the moral right under the Copyright, Designs and Patents Act 1988 to be identified as the author of this work.

All Rights reserved. No part of this publication may be reproduced, stored in a retrieval system or transmitted, in any form or by any means without the prior consent of the author, nor be otherwise circulated in any form of binding or cover other than that which it is published and without a similar condition being imposed on the subsequent purchaser.

**www.newgeneration-publishing.com**

New Generation Publishing

# Acknowledgment

To Mrs Solda Nkosingibhekile Nkosi, the world most brilliant mum who gave me love, strength and encouragement in the beginning up till now. To all my family: Mildred Lololo Nkosi, Bethwel Muziwenkosi Nkosi, Elizabeth Tiyoyo Nkosi, Dumisani Nkosi, Veronica Fikile Nkosi ,Dudu Thembelihle Nkosi, Jerome Jabulani Nkosi for their support. To my two adorable children: Madi Zoli Nkosi, Prince Sibusiso Gama for being good and supportive. To all my neighbours and everyone who played a part in my journey. Finally, I would like to thank David Ayodele for the support, encouragement and guidance he gave me throughout the trial of this book. I will always admired him as my dear friend.

I thank you all.


Princess Zanele Nkosi

# CONTENTS

CHAPTER 1  No Place like Home ............................. 1

CHAPTER 2  Our Dad's Attitude .............................. 3

CHAPTER 3  Financial Difficulties .......................... 6

CHAPTER 4  One Cow Went Missing ...................... 8

CHAPTER 5  Only On Tuesdays ............................ 10

CHAPTER 6  She Was a Good Mum ...................... 12

CHAPTER 7  On Christmas Day ............................. 13

CHAPTER 8  No Changes ....................................... 16

CHAPTER 9  Dark Cloud ......................................... 19

CHAPTER 10  Small Changes ................................ 21

CHAPTER 11  My Part Time Job ........................... 23

CHAPTER TWELVE  We Thank You Mum .......... 27

# CHAPTER 1

## No Place like Home

I was born and brought up in an old fashioned way, in rural area called Machibini under the King Mathonsi in South Africa. During those years, there were no gas or electricity in my area. I had three brothers and four sisters. I was a little girl in the family.

My dad spent most of his time away in the army. He occasionally came home. My mum was also staying at work place where she worked as a domestic worker. This means that all works were left to my elder sisters to take care of and manage the house. There were three separate rooms at home. The kitchen was one of the most important part of the house. We had a fire place at the centre of the kitchen where we gathered around it, while my eldest sisters did most of the house work. Inside the kitchen there was also two wooden shelves, one paraffin burning stove on the top of the first shelf. On the second shelf there were pots and dishes that were well arranged and organised.

I can remember that I was still young before I started school. I used to follow my sisters to the forest to collect woods and dried fallen branches to make open fire mainly to keep us warm during cold weather. We sometimes went to collect dry poo for cow as it made a real strong fire and last longer. In the kitchen we had a wooden window where you cannot see through outside unless you open them.

The kitchen would be filled with smoke from open fire but we never developed any kind of illness resulted from the thick smoke. It was funny but enjoyable to use newspapers as table clothes. Newspapers were also used to block any hole made by rats at the edges or corners of the house. During raining weather, we usually used open boxes as a door mat to get rid of mud from outside. Not a single room had cement floor, in that case we used cow poos to plaster the floor to get it freshened up.

When my mum was due to come home from work, my eldest sisters used to delegate work or task to be done so to please our mum like cleaning rooms, sweeping the whole yard, washing clothes, dishes and pots in more complex way using wood's ashes to shine them up. All my movement was always supervised so there would be no contamination until my mum arrives. We were delighted to get appraisal from our mum for the good house work we had done. That is what we were up to. Those appraisals made us feel great knowing that we got some skills of doing home task. Our self-esteem were boosted and shinning. Luckily, my eldest sisters were taught those skills by our mum while they were young. And we adopted those skills from them and we never ever thought of being over worked or abused. We were always happy and enjoyed every minutes.

The worst part of open fire which was centrally located in the Kitchen was that we sometimes found it really difficult to get it started in raining weather since woods would have been soaked. In that case, we used to add plastic bags and a drop of paraffin to get the fire started. Open fire was more useful because that was where we used to hold our wet clothes closer to the fire to dry them up. Though our clothes finally had a smoke perfume we did not bother with that.

We always work hand in hand with my sisters. We always understood the situation of mum being not at home and days were never the same but each and every day, we always had pre-planned tasks to deal with. It was never difficult for us as we were always happy, united and supportive of each other. We learned to understand and to take the situation as it was. We never failed.

# CHAPTER 2

## Our Dad's Attitude

Whenever my dad returns home from his army work, he used to call my youngest brother and myself more often to discuss some different issues. He sometimes patted both of our cheeks for any signs of stickiness that might indicate that we have been eaten sugar-cane. My dad was against the idea of eating sugar-cane to avoid catching cold as that was his belief.

He never considered any age differences among us and did not seems to be bothered whether you are young or grown up when it comes to task to be done. There were home policies and guidelines we had to make sure that we adhere to. The worst part of it was my dad never considered girls' education as a priority while my mum supports education for everyone in the family. Mum and Dad usually argued when it comes to educational issues. My dad did not want us as girls to go to school for education, he believed that one day all girls will be getting married and he will lose and not getting anything back.

Also he never called us by our names. Instead, he used to call out "Hey" expecting all of us to come and kneel in front of him. So, while we were still there kneeling down in front of him, we had to be quiet and wait for him to decide and select who he wanted among us. After selection, the rest would stand up and go back. It was a bit scary because during that moment we found the atmosphere very tense. Those years, we never ever thought of being abused or victimized. We were always happy despite. We used to put everything behind us and move on.

My dad was very strict to all of us especially the girls. He always got us (girls) involved in activities that should be done by my brothers. There were policies and procedures laid down by my dad to us as girls that we have to follow and stick to them in his presence or absence. We had no choice but to stick on those policies to indicate respect as he was our dad.

The strain of living and restrictions imposed by my dad while he was at home was really difficult such that one of my brother decided to run away from home. He went to live with other family about 3 miles away from home and he settled over there but only visited us if my dad was not around.

At home, the gate was to be locked at 6pm in that case everyone must be within the premises before that time. As my dad did not like the idea of girls to have education, he then allocated us to look after cows as our permanent job. He knew pretty well that we would not get any chance to attend classes. Once a week we (as girls) had to take cows to the deep. We had to find our own way on how we can get to school like all other children in my community. My mum was interested in us being educated but she had no power over my dad as she was only a wife. During those years, everything were ruled and controlled by a man as the head of the family as His words were final. Against my dad's rules, whenever he was not at home, we decided to leave cows hanging around and go to school. After school, we would go to collect the cows in the afternoon. Although, our school attendance was really poor. We sometimes missed some lessons while one of my middle sister (Fikile) had to stop attending school for one year to look after cows as they were increasing in numbers and causing problems in the community. Although, my dad gave Fikile one cow as a reward. That did not help her because she ended up being behind at school as compared to her age mate.

Whenever we bring cows at home from grazing field, he used to sit by Kraal gate on his small chair to count each and every cow that goes passed in front of him and observe whether the cows are full up. He always told us that he has skills to assess if the cow is full up or hungry.

We sometimes found ourselves being beaten up by my dad telling us that cows were not well fed. The following day, we were told to take cows to the area with rich green grass and stay over there all day meaning that we would not be able to attend classes during that day. We always accept the situation as it was. If one cow gone missing, we were not allowed to sleep in the house. We had to walk around at night in the dark looking for the missing cow.

Although, I cannot remember exactly who made such arrangement but we ended up attending morning classes because after mid-day, we had a responsibility to bring the cows back home and milk them. Milking time was due strictly at 1pm every day until the cow grows up.

All teachers at school knew and understood our situation as it was already reported to them that sometimes we would not be able to attend classes. We always missed some lessons but whenever we got a chance to be at school, we picked up as much as we could. Our teachers were great and really helpful.

Each time we got home from school, we had to look for something to eat before we went to collect cows from grazing field. Getting something to eat was not a big issue since we had a big garden where we cultivated some vegetables. Due to that, we were really young for this job of looking after cows. So, sometimes while we were out at grazing field, we ended up forgetting and start a game of climbing up trees, fishing tadpoles and chasing each other.

The moment it got darker, that was the time we started to remember that we have to collect cows and go home. Sometimes, we found that cows were separated far from each other and that makes it difficult to bring them together.

# CHAPTER 3

# Financial Difficulties

There was never enough money to meet our school needs since we were only supported by our mum for education. She was not earning enough money where she worked. Despite that, our class teachers were patient in case we paid school fees a bit late. As we come from different families, most children at school were always wearing school shoes and socks but in my family we did not have enough money to buy shoes and socks like other school mates

We were always behind with everything. Sometimes, we could not manage to buy all books needed at school. We kept borrowing from other children. At school there was a policy stated that if you did not pay full school fees, you would not get results at the end of the term until you pay the balance. Most of the time, we got our results when schools are starting. That was the time one could find out whether you passed or failed.

During Christmas time, while all kids were happy with their results, we were stuck in the middle about unknown results. We put everything and all hope to our mum. We always hope that she will get some money to pay school fees balance and get our result.

As we all understand the circumstances in the family, we never mentioned or talked about school trip knowing that mum would not have money to pay for school trip as she was struggling to pay our school fees hence why we never put pressure on her. We never got upset about that either. Our aim was only "to get education". We were really good kids and we were not hanging around with bad crowds.

Though, my dad made some contributions in buying food, but he was not aware that we were going to school.

And since dad was not responsible for our education, all responsibilities of school fees, school uniforms was on our Mum. At this point, she had given up persuading my dad for school financial assistance. Mum was a very strong woman, she was brave, and she was loving mother to her children. She was always positive and she never failed.

# CHAPTER 4

## One Cow Went Missing

One day my dad was at home from the army. We took all cows for grazing as usual and in the afternoon, we started to collect them to go home. Unfortunately, we could not find one cow. It went missing and since were aware of the family policy, we headed home with the rest of the cows and we had to go back to look for missing cow. It was really dark and could hardly see ahead. It was with my middle sister that evening.

I had no idea where we were going to but our conversation was all about where to go first to find the missing cow. We walked a long distance but there was no trace of the missing cow. It was getting darker and darker. We ended up inside the forest still looking for the missing cow. We could not see it. As we knew that my dad would not let us in the house until we find the missing cow, we then found a big rock where we decided to sit under that rock until the following day. We curled ourselves without any blanket. It was really scary because that area under the rock could be a hideout for dangerous animals especially at night. We had nothing to eat that night. We kept whispering all-night, we never slept a wink as we were frightened. We had no option but to curl under the rock. In the morning, we carried on with our search.

Now, in the morning, we remembered that there was one family miles away who had many cows like ours. We thought the missing cow could be there, so we went to that family to find out. Fortunately, the missing cow was there. We collected it and headed home to collect the rest of them grazing on the field. On that same day, we missed our lessons at school. Although, we were used to it. Amazingly, we never hated our dad. We accepted everything as it was. We were lucky because the strain and pressure have never changed our behaviour towards our parents. We always adore them and admired them equally.

# CHAPTER 5

## Only On Tuesdays

Tuesday was the most exciting day of the week. This was the only day when my mum would come home from work to see us. We took this day as a special and blessing day of our lives. Every Tuesday, when it started to get darker, we gathered and curling ourselves by the road waiting for our mum to arrive. We knew that her place of work was about 3 hours walking distance away. This was one of the reasons she could not travel every day.

We seated there along the road wondering on how far my mum was. We were concerned about any dangers she would have come across with while walking on her own in the dark. There was no buses available during that time of the day. There was nobody to tell us on how far she was. We kept bending down to see if there is any shade that resembled human being. There was no means to communicate like telephone. We never gave up, we never lost hope that our mum would finally arrive. We kept re-assuring each other throughout. We were scared to walk in the dark to meet her half way. We had hope that she was on her way home.

There were no cars passing along the road since there were no many cars around my area. It was really a poor community. There was only one bus running during the day and finished early afternoon. Sometimes, I felt tears rolling down my cheeks as it was dark and nobody noticed anything. We never stopped saying that our mum is on her way, she might be getting closer and closer. We only became restless and started panicking when we noticed that time is gradually running out, but we never gave up. Finally our mum arrived home.

We knew that she always comes home carrying a box on her head with bread and jam. She also brought old newspapers to sell them at our local shop. As soon as my mum got home, she sometimes told us that there were visitors at her work place so she had to clean up and leave everything in place before she was allowed to leave. Mum was working very hard for survival especially to get money for our education. We enjoyed every moment while our mum was at home. We knew that was going to be a short period of time before leaving back to her place of work. We got used to it.

The following day mum would get up very early while it was still dark headed to work. Sometimes, I got up and to find that she was gone. We never ever questioned our mum about the kind of life we were living. Both our parents brought us in religious way. We never forgot to pray before we went to sleep despite their absence.

# CHAPTER 6

## She Was a Good Mum

It was really funny that our mum never discussed with us about getting married but she always told us about the importance of education in our lives. I can remember that my mum never attended a single parents meeting at school because she was not at home. She never received any complaints about us from school as well. Our neighbours were brilliant. They would attend school meeting and passed any relevant information to our mum when she got home. Our neighbour never left us behind, they were there for us. We did not feel lonely as neighbours were supportive.

My mum always told us about good behaviour as she was always pleased with our school results though she never got time to help out with school work. She was not at home. My mum sometimes told us about her family history and how she was brought up by her dad. Unfortunately, my mum never knew her mum. My grandmother passed away while my mum was still a kid. My mum was brought up in a strong positive way. She never presented to us emotional face and she never told us about any difficulties she came across with on daily basis. She was simple and straight forward. She got on so well with all our neighbours and there was no arguments among them. We were all united.

# CHAPTER 7

## On Christmas Day

This was our most special day with local neighbours. Sometimes our mum would be lucky to be at home during Christmas day. Before Christmas day our family used to be invited by mum's employer to go there and collect our Christmas presents. My eldest sisters knew the direction to get there. We had to leave home very early in the morning to walk because it was a long distance. One week prior our visits, we used to start preparing couple of songs for entertainments

During our journey, we used to take breaks under the trees especially if it is a sunning day as we had a long way to go. We had no money to catch the bus, we did not bother with that. In fact, we could not felt that hardest walk because sometimes we kept chasing each other throughout the way until we got there. We were delighted and interested to get there as soon as possible. The moment we got in, there would be crowds of neighbours and friends invited to join the party. The party was set up in the garden where everything was well arranged for the party to begin. After couple of minutes that the party started, we were called to sing and play drum majorettes using empty box as drum kit. The crowd were really delighted and enjoyed it. In between breaks we had drinks and cakes. It was the time where each of us were handed rapped present and few amount of money as our Christmas presents. Among presents, we had dress of different floral colours. While my brother was presented with short and T-shirt. We had fun all day. Due to long journey home, we had to leave very early in the afternoon. We were really happy with our presents because we know our mum would not afford to buy them. We were like millionaires with that few money. It meant a lot to us.

In our local community we used to have Christmas party held in one family house locally. That was where we were going to show off our new dress. We received invitations 3-4 weeks in advanced to get enough time to do rehearsal and to prepare Christmas presents to our friends. We formed a group with local friends to practice songs knowing that it would be a singing competition and drama. We wanted to make sure our performance took first price in the competitions.

It was a huge operation during preparation because everyone wanted to look much better in front of the audience. The worst part was, we had no shoes to wear during that special day. I can say nighty-five percent of the youth in my area had no shoes to wear in the party. Others had only a pair of school shoes that cannot be worn to this party. In that case, we had to start searching for old shoes in neighbours' gardens. And sometimes, we were lucky to find one old shoe that was already bent and hard like a rock due to long exposure to sun and rain. That type of shoe was impossible to recognize whether it was for right or left foot. The good thing was that some of these old shoes fitted most of us.

We continued with our search for another shoe to make a pair. One friend would find one shoe and only to find those shoes are not pairs. As long as both shoes had same colour that was good enough despite the differences in sizes, we then sat down and start fitting them. Due to their hardness, they fitted all of us. If it happened that a pair of shoe was found by different people, it means that that shoe belong to both of them. We arranged and agreed that during party day, first person is going to wear them during first performance. Then around the midday, another person had to wear it but only those people who found each pair of shoes. It did not matter to us even if we had to swap same pair of shoes by couple of people in the same day at the same party.

During performances, even if you feel a bit discomfort on your shoe due to hardness that person had to be patient not to interfere with any kind of movement in front of the audience until the song is finished. Once you are outside, is the time you sort out.

We used red shoe polish as lipsticks, we also used wood ashes as face powder. The worst part of ashes was that if it had been raining, it would be wet and it would not do the job. In that case, we cooked candles mixed with paraffin and let it boiled, after that we allowed it to cool down before using. We then applied to our face to get it puffy. The smell was horrible, it was our number one homemade face product. We wrapped glasses, plates, spoons, cups and other different items using newspapers for Christmas presents to friends. Sometimes, we took my mum's items from home, folded them and write our names on them so that our names would be called out now and again and people think that we received many presents and you are well known.

After the party is over, we went home and make sure that we unwrapped all my mum's items and put them back in their places. All these was due to lack of money to buy Christmas present. We were more than happy by doing that. It was all funny to us but we enjoyed every moment of it. We never wanted that special day to end.

# CHAPTER 8

## No Changes

In the family, we had a small radio that my mum bought for us but we were not allowed by our dad to listen to it. My dad did not like the noise from radio. It was turned off throughout until my dad is gone back to work. Also, laughing very loudly was prohibited in the family. I was always the target of being beaten by my dad for laughing very loud causing horrible noise to him. My sisters used to crack a joke and we started laughing but sometimes, I was unable to control my laughter. My dad always recognised my laughter from a distance as his bedroom was not far from the kitchen where we used to crack jokes.

There was always something strange with our dad because if he had planned to punish one of us, he could not do it same time but he will let us go to sleep as if nothing was wrong. Around 2am, he would come to our bedroom with a touch light on his hand bearing in mind that it was dark at night. So, he will quickly spot the person he wanted to punish. In some cases, he would grab whoever he came across first and asked for the person he wanted. You had to make your mind up quickly and respond very quickly before you get into trouble. He did that on purpose to punish us during that time of the night. He knew that we would not be able to run away outside as it was still very dark.

While my dad was at home from work, news would spread very quickly to our neighbours that he is at home. Neighbours did report to each other and messages were passed to all our local friends. After that there would be no a single visitor or neighbour coming in to our house. People kept themselves at a distance until my dad has gone to work but that did not mean he was a bad person. The truth was that he did not like many people around him except his family. He was really good to us. He sometimes called us, and we would sit in front of him and he would sing different songs to us that he learnt in the army from his mates. He also told us stories and things going on the army. At times, other stories were scary and sometimes we found it difficult to believe and to understand.

My dad had many different medals that he used to spread in front of us and explained to us on how he got each and every medal as a reward for his good job he has done in the army. To us it was difficult to understand the meaning of each medal. We were expecting to see trophies as medals that we were familiar with.

Since we were living between two neighbours, there was a short route from one neighbour to another that went via to our family yard. While my dad was at home, that route always became temporary out of use until my dad is gone to work. All neighbours were really scared of my dad as it seems that he was unapproachable man but with no specific reason. People kept at a distance as much as they can.

Army truck used to come to drop and pick him up to work. After he was gone, we felt like we were in a different planet. As I had mentioned before that while he was at home, the gate was locked up at 6pm. If you were sent somewhere far away from home, you would have to run as much as your leg could carry you to be home before 6pm. When you arrived home after that time, you would have to stand outside the gate and call out for help. The keys were kept by our dad. The bundles of keys were attached to his belt. The gate keys had to be requested from him to let that person in. As soon as you got in you had to answer endless questions from him about late coming before you are freed.

Every afternoon after the gate was locked he had a tendency of calling us one by one to come to him. You would not come on behalf of someone else no matter how busy that person was. That was the strategy he used to count us. Early in the morning around 4am - 5am, my dad would walk around the yard to check the fence for any suspicion that someone had jumped out of the fence overnight. We took this as part of protection other than being abused or restrained. My dad was over protective but we were happy with that.

There was a big shed at home separated from all other rooms where my dad kept all his home working equipment. That shed was always locked at all times. Inside the shed my dad had a small can that was stuffed with money. That can with money inside was buried in the ground at the centre on the floor.

Nobody knew how much was there. Even my mum had no access into it. Only my dad who controlled it. No matter how things were, we never attempted to take it out. He kept counting that money now and again while he was at home. I would not be sure whether he had any bank book. He was very secretive to some other issues.

# **CHAPTER 9**

# Dark Cloud

I had no idea whether my dad was on annual leave or sick leave. I remembered that there was a time where he came home and stayed in for a longer period of time than he used to. His presence was a little bit tough to us though as we noticed remarkable changes in his mobility. He was less mobile. He spent most of his time laid in bed.

Our mum also started to spend more days at home other than at work place. I was told that my dad is at home because he was unwell. I was not sure on what was wrong with him. Also, I heard that my mum was there to look after him. During those years, I had no idea about any serious medical conditions. I was told that my dad suffer from asthma. He did not walk a long distance but home policies never changed. Despite of his reduced mobility, he was still capable of keeping close eyes on cows than ever. He loved his cows than anything.

My dad was in bed on this particular day while my mum asked me to go and call one of my eldest sister although she did not mention any reason for that. I noticed that my mum was in tears as soon as I got back to my mum with my sister, we started to move some items outside to create more space inside my dad's room. I had no idea on what was going on. It was not long before the room was full of neighbours. They started to sing church songs. I went to the kitchen to join some of my sisters and that was the time they told me that my dad had passed away. It was really difficult moment to the whole family. I had no idea on what to do at that moment and my sisters were crying also. I was not allowed to go and sit next to my mum.

During the day, we were told that we are not allowed to go to school the following day until my dad was buried. I really did like the idea of having couple of days off school especially during the cold days and I would not need to do homework. There was no need to get up in the morning preparing for school. I did not bother missing lessons at school during this period.

The preparation for my dad's funeral was sorted. The following day, he was buried in the graveyard far away from home. I did not think that I would not see him again. I had some misunderstanding and was confused. Time arrived where we had to go back to school. All teachers and friends were very supportive towards us. They showed sympathy. My mum had to stop working completely and to stay at home with us. It was heart breaking to lose our dad but we gradually became stronger and stronger.

# CHAPTER 10

## Small Changes

As my mum had to leave her permanent job and stay at home. Fortunately, she was talented in dressmaking. She had a sewing machine where she did her sewing job. She had no training or qualifications but she had lots of experiences in sewing. People used to bring some clothes to be sewed or amended. She was brilliant in sewing wedding gowns and school uniforms. That was the only way she could get money for our education. The school uniforms were in high demand especially at the beginning of each school year.

One of my eldest sister had part time job somewhere in the town. My sister (Fikile) who once left school for one year looked after cows. She was about to finish high school. Unfortunately, there was no enough money for her to go for further education. Because of that she had to look for job and she found a job in one of the local factories (Kwa-sithebe). I was still in high school with one of my sister then. Those who had job were really helpful in the family. They made some financial contribution, helping out with everything. My Mum continued with her sewing job until she bought us black and white television.

The number of children came to watch the television started to increase in number. We started to charge 2p per person. That was the other means of raising money as a family. We also use that money to take the battery to local garage to be charged. Things got slowly better and better. There were some remarkable changes. We were no longer kids, we had to work very hard to get family going.

At school, I was selling some sandwiches to get money for school needs. My sister, Dudu, who was still at school also had to sell some different items like sweets and cakes though her business usually collapsed now and again because we sometimes got tempted and eat most of it. Her selling business was on and off. We used to help each to re-start business. Our mum tried to make us look and feel good like all other school mates, though it was a bit of struggle but she managed with our help. We were united and we shared everything equally. More changes were contributed by my sister who had a job. She started to have more clothes and couple of pair of shoes that we shared among us. The journey to the garden looking for shoes came to an end.

We were still not actually involved in school trips, though things were not exactly the same as before. We started to join school trip only if we were part of the team. I was a netball player as well as athlete. In that case, the family worked together contributing money for me to go to school trip. Wood ashes as face powder also came to an end. My eldest sister had started buying ponds cream that we all shared. We were a bit grown up to understand that shoe polish should not be used as lip stick.

My mum also did not like or support the idea of using shoe polish as a lip stick. That was not the way we were brought up. She tried to direct us to the way she was brought up of which was good. I did not know and I cannot remembered what happened about cows at home. Their number got less and less until they all finished. I believed that everything has got its start and its end.

# CHAPTER 11

# My Part Time Job

We were all willing and interested to make some financial contributions to meet family needs. While I was still in high school, it was too much school work to do but I was doing very well. My mind never got discouraged about the status of the family. I just forgot and put everything behind and concentrate on my study.

I decided to start looking for part time job to work weekend to get money. Those years, you had to get school permit from your principal that allows you to work. As soon as I got my school permit, I started to look around for weekend jobs. One day, I was with my local friend and we discussed about finding job. She was also interested to get work. We then remembered that there was a lorry that used to pass along with girls on board. The lorry used to come back in the afternoon around 5pm.

My friend and I agreed to meet at a certain area that following morning to board lorry. We did not know the lorry driver and he did not know us but we just flagged down the lorry. It stopped and we boarded without any word. He drove off, we only discussed with the girls at the back of the lorry on what we were up to. The girls re-assured us that it is never a problem to get this kind of Job. They also told us that they were always short staffed. It sounded great to us. So, we knew pretty well that we had found what we were looking for.

We arrived in the main office of the company. The office was an old building surrounded by sugar cane field. My friend and I were introduced by girls to the supervisor. The supervisor did not ask any paper. No forms were filled up, no proof of identity were needed, and no pay rate was discussed. No contract to be agreed and signed. It was a bit strange because we were not asked to produce even school permit. We asked the girls on how are we going to know that we have been offered a job. The girls told us that it was not the problem to get this kind of job. The supervisor came around and he gave us hoe blade. That indicated that we were being offered a job. We did not know about salary and payday.

On my wrist, I had a watch that did not work at all. It was there as jewellery. I was asked by the supervisor to remove my wrist watch. He continued telling us the work policy that there is no employee allowed to have watch. He asked me to hand it over to him and promised to give it back after work. He took it despite explaining that does not work. The supervisor continued saying we as employee are not allowed to know what time was during working hours. He said, he is the one who indicate the tea break and lunch break. That was strange and funny. To me it was clear on why we were not allowed to know the time of the day.

The job was the same to everyone. There was no senior position except supervisor though there were couple of girls who were highly experienced. Our job was to remove weeds in between sugar canes. We were then taken by a tractor from the office to work area. There were huge yards of sugar cane. We were allocated each 5 lines that was expected to be done before the end of the shift. I was new to this job with no experience. I was always left behind but the girls were supportive. They came around to help me and showed me on how to do it in a quicker way. It was really hot day. Everyone was sweating due to hot weather and kind of job we were doing. The sugar cane lines were long to such that you could not see where it ended.

I kept working on and on. I was really exhausted. The supervisor told us to keep working none-stop until he blew the whistle to indicate break time. The day sometimes can tell what time it is. The whistle we were waiting for did not go off, we kept going with our work. At last we heard the whistle.

During break time, the company brought in something

to eat. I was not interested and familiar with what they were serving. I seated down to get some rest without anything with me to eat because I was not sure if I would get the job. We all seated down for our break in an open area with no trees for shade panicking about whistle that would go off at any time as indication to get back to work. It was horrible, I was hungry but had no choice because I needed money.

While we were waiting for that whistle, it went off and we got back to work and continued with job from where we ended. Those with experience were far away with their allocated lines. I got scratched on my leg and arms from sugar cane and that pain and itchy kept disturbing throughout.

The supervisor was not that bad. He kept following behind us sometimes laughing. He noticed that I had less experience in this kind of job. We carried on in that sunny day looking forward to lunch time. I once thought of leaving the job (re-signing) but there was no chance as there was not transport to go back home. I had no idea on where I was.

The whistle went off to indicate lunch time but I did not fancy what they offered me for lunch. Our lunch were loaded in black plastic bin brought in by tractor. These plastic bins loaded more enough food for staff. The company did not have proper containers as bread were stuffed in sacks. After lunch, we carried on working until 5pm and that was the time to go home. The tractor was already around to collect us to the office where lorry was ready to transport us home.

There were many questions to answer on our way home. Girls kept asking us if we love the job, whether we will come back next Saturday. We promised them that we did not mind doing that kind of job though. They doubted us.

At home, I told my sisters on how was the job and about whistle blowing by supervisor. We all laughed. It was funny and interesting story. I was looking forward to tell my friend at school about my part time job. As soon as I told my friend, they were not interested with the job at all. They laughed. The issue of not allowed to know time while working did raise some speculations to everyone.

The following Saturday, I decided to continue with my job though there was a bit of hesitation. I finally found how to enjoy it. The supervisor was good, no pressure from him. While working, employees were allowed to talk to each other, laughing and singing very loud. After the school was closed. I decided to work permanent from Monday to Friday. Friday was our pay day. We started work from 8am and finished at 5pm.

My Salary made a huge difference in the family. Every Friday, we knocked-off a bit earlier so the lorry can drop us in the town to do some shopping. The lorry driver used to set up specific time where we should be back in the same area to be taken home.

On one occasion, all netball players had a trip to compete with other team far away from our area. I used my savings to pay bus fee. I felt great because I was able to raise the money on my own in order to reduce pressure on our mum.

# CHAPTER TWELVE

## We Thank You Mum

Mum, you were not always with us at home and we understood clearly well your absence was not because of being neglected or abused but you were working very hard so we could get good education. We were happy, we all had one ambition. Mum, you brought us up in religious belief that you passed on to us. In your absence we never forgot to pray before we went to sleep. Mum, we understood how much difficulties and challenges you came across but you never showed it in your emotions or attitudes towards us.

Mum, you did not have the opportunity to listen to our end of the year school results due to your work, and we are grateful for all your supports throughout. Neighbours were very supportive of us too while you were away. They always treated us the same as their children. There was no magic in it but the fact was you wanted us to have a successful life. While you were at home, you were committed and dedicated to us. You made sure that we were comfortable, happy and settled. Mum, we never lost sight of the fact that despite what was happening to our lives, it was really nothing as compared to other families where kids never attended school despite of their parent's advice and encouragements.

Mum, you never owed anybody any penny to help us with education. You were always focussed, you had lots of patience and you were strong than ever. In the end, you made it, you mastered and you had such strong strength. Mum, your criticisms were always constructive. You really changed our lives forever. Our dreams come true. We love you, adore you and admired you. You deserve a lot from all of your children. We owe you mum something that we will never pay back in total.

Mum, you are our hero!